Level 3
Beginning Reader

Book 1: Focusing on reading three-letter "a" words and a short story

Amanda Riccetti

illustrations by Steven Gomez

Library of Congress Control Number: 2015919631

Published in the United States by CreateSpace Independent Publishing Platform,
a DBA of On-Demand Publishing LLC, an Amazon Company, South Carolina.

www.createspace.com

www.bigcitymontessorischool.com

Big City Publishing is a registered trademark of Big City Montessori School.

Library of Congress Cataloging-in-Publication Data

Riccetti, Amanda, 2016 —

Reading with Miss Amanda, Book 1 ; Level 1 Yellow – Pre-reader
by Amanda Riccetti; illustrations by Steven Gomez

p. cm.

Summary: In the Level 1 Yellow series, Miss Amanda uses phonetic learning
to teach 15 letters using the Montessori three-part lesson.

ISBN 13:978-1548409104 | ISBN 10: 1548409103

Design by Robert Riccetti

Printed in the United States of America

This book is dedicated to every child who wants to learn how to read, and the adult in their life who wants to support them.

Contents

What to expect

PHONETIC LEARNING: Throughout this series, children learn letter sound recognition. In the Montessori method, we do not call letters "ABC" but rather refer to their sound. For example, the letter "i" is called "ih" as in "ih-gloo" and the letter "a" is called "ah" as in "apple." Remember to always call letters by their sounds.

INTUITIVE LESSONS: The lessons in the "Reading with Miss Amanda" series will feel completely intuitive to children, even if they have different styles of learning. The illustrations and games help to engage younger children at the beginning, then evolve into appealing exercises that will teach your child to read.

TIME SPENT: Expect to spend about 10-20 minutes per day on the book, for 5 days a week. Each book could take as little as 1 week to master, or up to 2 months, depending on the pace of the child and the level the child is on.

REPETITION IS GOOD: Children love repetition, and it drives learning. For example, the popular book "Goodnight Moon" by Margaret Wise Brown might bore an adult, but children love the repetition of phrases. So if you use this book and think, "that's repetitive," remember - it's been designed that way.

If you have any issues, go to the FAQs at the end of the book.

Reading with Miss Amanda

5 levels (5 books per level)

	Typical Age*	Reading level**	Example
L 1	3+ Pre-Reader	Has not learned letter sounds yet	"ah", "buh," "cuh"
L 2	4+ Becoming a Reader	Has not learned to phonetically read three-letter words yet	"Max," "rat," "cat"
L 3	4+ Becoming a Reader	Has not learned to read short sentences yet	"The crab ran and hid."
L 4	4+ Becoming a Reader	Has not learned to read four- or five-letter words in short sentences yet	"The crab ran on the sand."
L 5	5+ Advance Reader	Has not learned silent vowels (cake) or blended vowels (oo, ai) yet	"The cook baked a cake."

*The ages listed are merely guidelines that Montessori teachers use as a basis to introduce reading lessons.

**The series is also ideal for older children who need to learn reading, or children with a learning difference, such as dyslexia.

Hi there! Welcome back to my class! In this book you will find lessons that will help you learn to read. Practice makes permanent.

Come join me!

Lesson 1
Reading and Matching

Tip

When your child comes across a letter he or she has not learned yet, or if they forget the letter, read the sound and continue. Through the repetition, he/she will learn the letters.

The first letter in this word makes the sound "vah".
Now read "v-aaaa-n" and find the match.

van

The first letter in this word makes the sound "yah". Now read "y- aaaaaa-m" and find the match. You did it! Let's continue!

yam

cap

You really are getting the hang of this.

ram

fan

cat

You reached your goal.

bat

Lesson 2

Reading Cards

Tip

Remember that you can stop at the end of any lesson, and can repeat or restart a lesson at any time. Just follow your child's natural pace!

max

You reached your goal.

has

You really are getting the hang of this.

fat

rat

Look at you reading!

hat

Nice !

sat

23

You got it.

van

pan

Nice work.

ant

yam

You reached your goal.

zag

In order to maintain your child's interest in the task and ability to continue learning, you will need to follow your child's pace. "Stop" pages are a reminder to offer your child a break if needed.

- Read Option A if you think it is time for a break, and Option B if your child appears interested in continuing.

- It is common for children to forget something they have just learned, so when you return, review the past lesson before starting the next one.

Lesson 3
Reading a word list

Tip

Remember that you can stop at the end of any lesson, and can repeat or restart a lesson at any time. Just follow your child's natural pace!

fan

zag

bag

bad

sad

wag

rat

pan

jab

fan

wax

fat

cat

ran

sat

zap

nap

sap

can

mad

van

man

yam

jam

Lesson 4

Reading short sentences

Tip

Sight words are words that can't easily be sounded out
and that appear frequently when we are reading.

The man is sad.

A yam in a pan.

The van is tan.

The bad ram.

The cat is mad.

The rat had a nap.

The ham is fat.

The ant ran.

Lesson 5

Reading a short story

Tip

Sight words are words that can't easily be sounded out and that appear frequently when we are reading.

Max has a cat.

Max has a fat cat.

Max has a rat.

Max has a fat rat.

Max sat on a hat.

The fat cat sat on Max.

The fat rat sat on the cat.

Max has a cat and a rat.

Great Job!

Congratulations! Your reached your goal. You completed pink book 1. This golden coin is for you. Keep up the hard work and I look forward to seeing you in the next book!

Accomplishments

The stamp is a symbol of your hard work. When you complete stamps for all the levels you will be an advanced reader.

L 1 — Book 1 · Book 2 · Book 3 · Book 4 · Book 5

L 2 — Book 1

L 3

L 4

L 5

FAQ

How much time should I spend on the book?

- Daily repetition is the best way to learn new information. If you skip days, you may end up repeating past lessons.

- An ideal schedule would be at least 5 times a week, for about 20 minutes per session.

Do I have to read the whole book?

- No. You can stop at the end of any lesson and restart at any time.

- You can also restart at any point in the book, depending on how well your child has grasped each lesson.

Is it ok to skip a section?

- Yes - if your child has mastered a section, keep working on the other sections that are still challenging.

What should I do when my child completes a lesson?

- FOLLOW THE CHILD - Ask your child if he/she would like to have another lesson. If he/she says "yes", then continue. This indicates your child is still interested and enjoying their time with you.

When is my child ready for the next book?

In the back of this book are words lists that you can review before advancing to the next book. When your child can read the words and the short story with ease, he/she is ready to advance to the next book. Remember, this is a marathon, not a race..

What are the 5 core skills my child needs to learn in order to read?

- Decoding: sounding out words

- Vocabulary and comprehension of the English language

- Rules of the English language

- Memory and attention

What if my child is having trouble sounding out the words?

- Read the word slowly and stretch out the middle sound, e.g., c-aaaaa-t. Have your child try the sound with you. Then have your child try again on their own.

- If your child is still struggling, I highly encourage you to go back to the orange level and build words. This revisit to practice building words will help your child hear the first, middle, and ending sounds of words.

- Remember, children often forget how to do something new, and your child may take from 1 week to as long as 1 month to master reading the words with ease.

What should I do if my child can't read words in a row?

Have your child read one word at a time while moving their finger under each word as they read. Then, read the sentence slowly while moving their finger under each word. Read the same sentence until your child can string the words together. The process is new and unfamiliar to your child. With practice, your child will read sentences.

FAQ

? What should I do if my child is having trouble focusing?

- TIME - Recognize your child may need breaks. Take a break after five minutes. Over time, slowly expand the time and the lesson.

- REPEAT - When you return, start at the beginning of the lesson - repeating something familiar builds confidence. Each time, the child will go further and further. When this lesson is easy, your child will be ready for the next challenge.

? Should my child practice writing as well as reading?

Yes! Reading and writing go hand in hand. To write a word, children have to "hear" it. Writing the words will help associate the sounds they hear with a letter. Words are made of sounds that are written with letters.

? Should I stop to explain when my child asks a question?

If your child has any questions about English-language rules, feel free to explain them as you go along. Example: "Mommy, why does the word 'rats' have an 's' at the end?" "Well, when there is more than one rat, you add an 's' at the end."

? What if my child doesn't know the definition of a word?

Reading also requires comprehension, so to build your child's vocabulary, the books offer words your child may not be familiar with yet. Explain to your child the definitions of words as they come up.

How can we integrate lessons into life?

- SENTENCE BOOKS - Children love reading about themselves. Write short sentences with your child's name, pet's name, friends, etc., and make personal books.

- DICTATION - When dictating, only use the sounds of the letters, e.g., "cah - ah- tuh spells cat." Use the word lists provided in the back of the book for dictation.

- EXTENSIONS - Help your child to further experience the concepts of the lessons. Have your child copy words and sentences they are learning from the book. Then have your child read them back to you. Practice makes permanent.

Why we only use lowercase letter sounds for dictation.

From a literacy perspective, to write and read, children need to learn the sounds letters make first. Once the phonetic reading skills are mastered, the names of letters are later used for spelling.

What is dyslexia?

Dyslexia is the most common reason children struggle when learning to read. It manifests differently for every child, and can range from mild to severe. At least 10% of the population is dyslexic. This book is your tool to support your child; it is particularly effective in helping dyslexic children learn to read.

fan	rat
zag	pan
bag	jab
bad	fan
sad	wax
wag	fat

cat	can
ran	mad
sat	van
zap	man
nap	yam
sap	jam

Made in the USA
San Bernardino, CA
29 November 2018